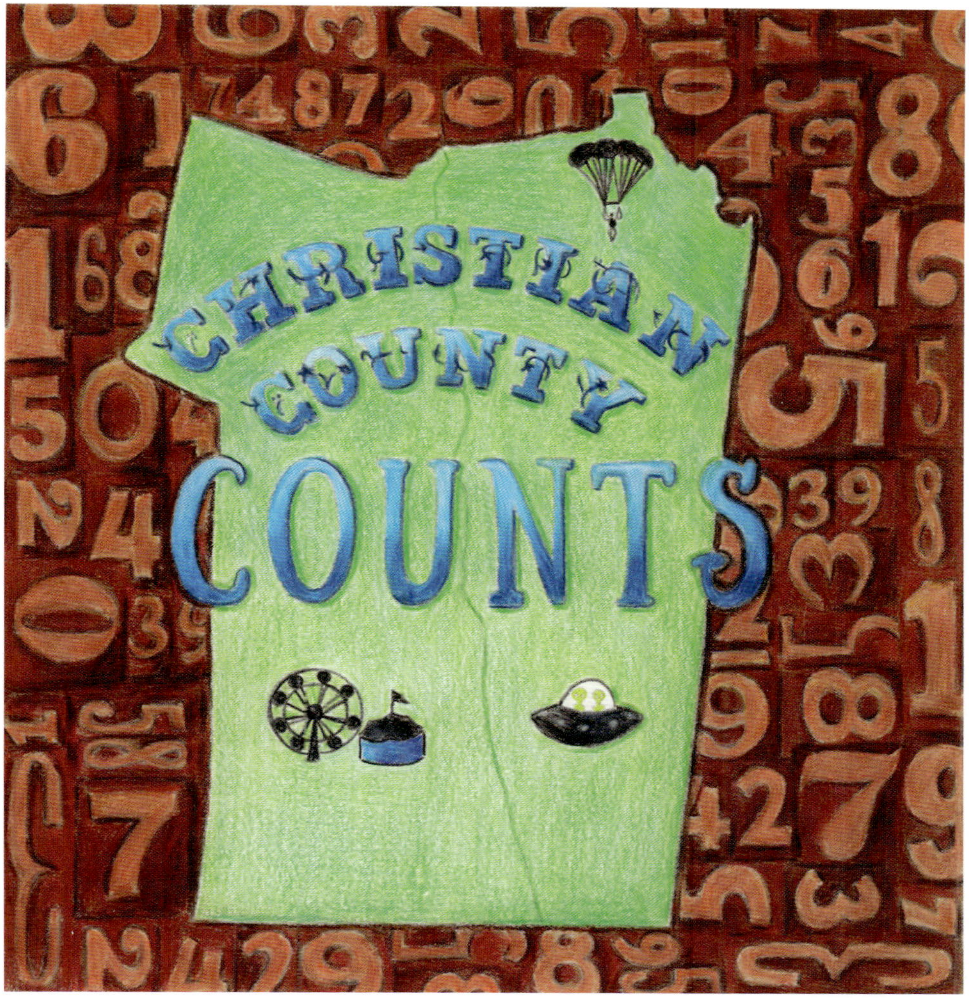

ISBN: 978-0-692-53790-9
Christian County Counts
1st Edition

Printed in the USA

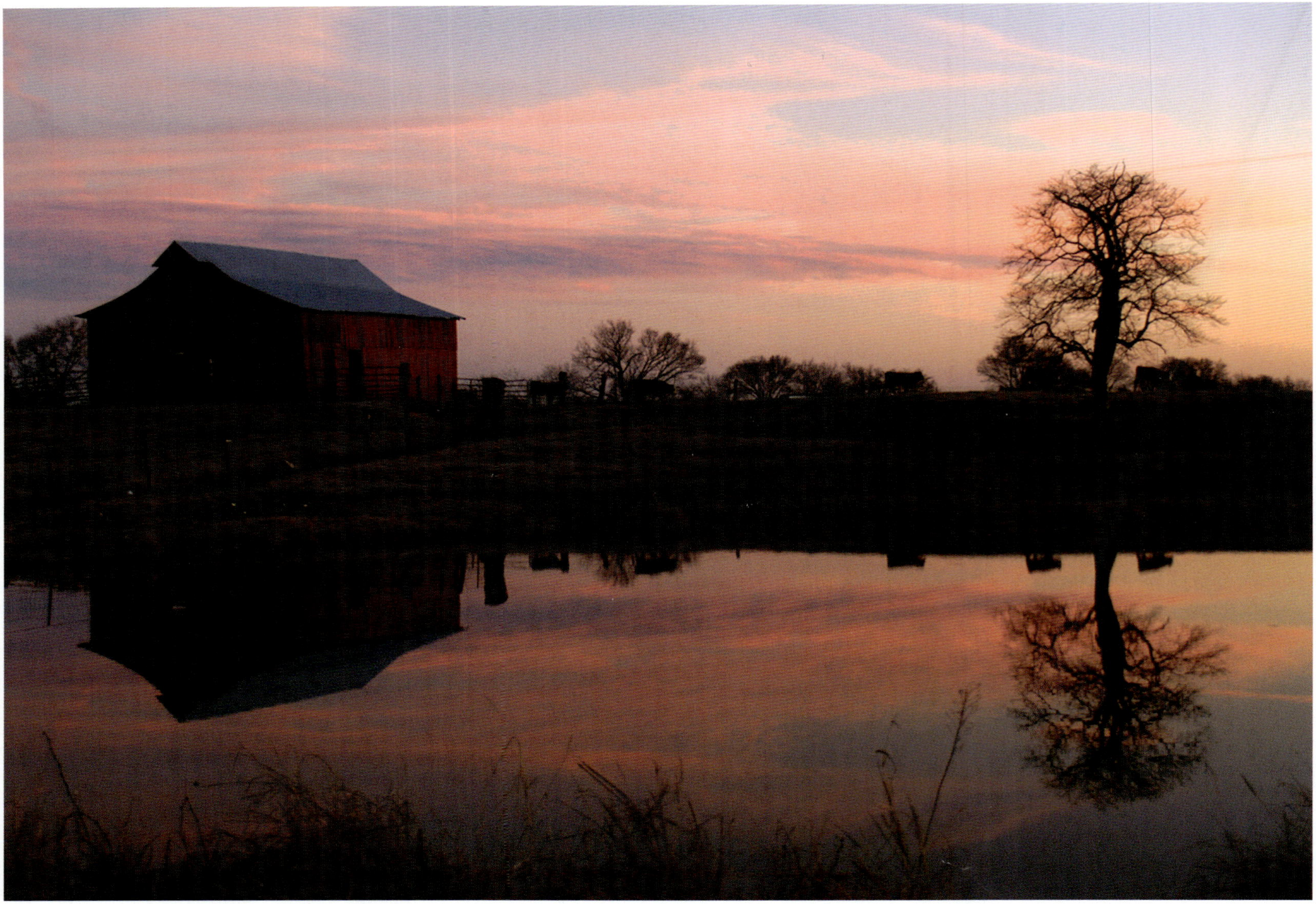

1

There is only 1 Christian County Kentucky, a special place we call home. What makes our county unique?

Murray Blake, artist

Sponsored By Christian County Convention and Visitors Bureau

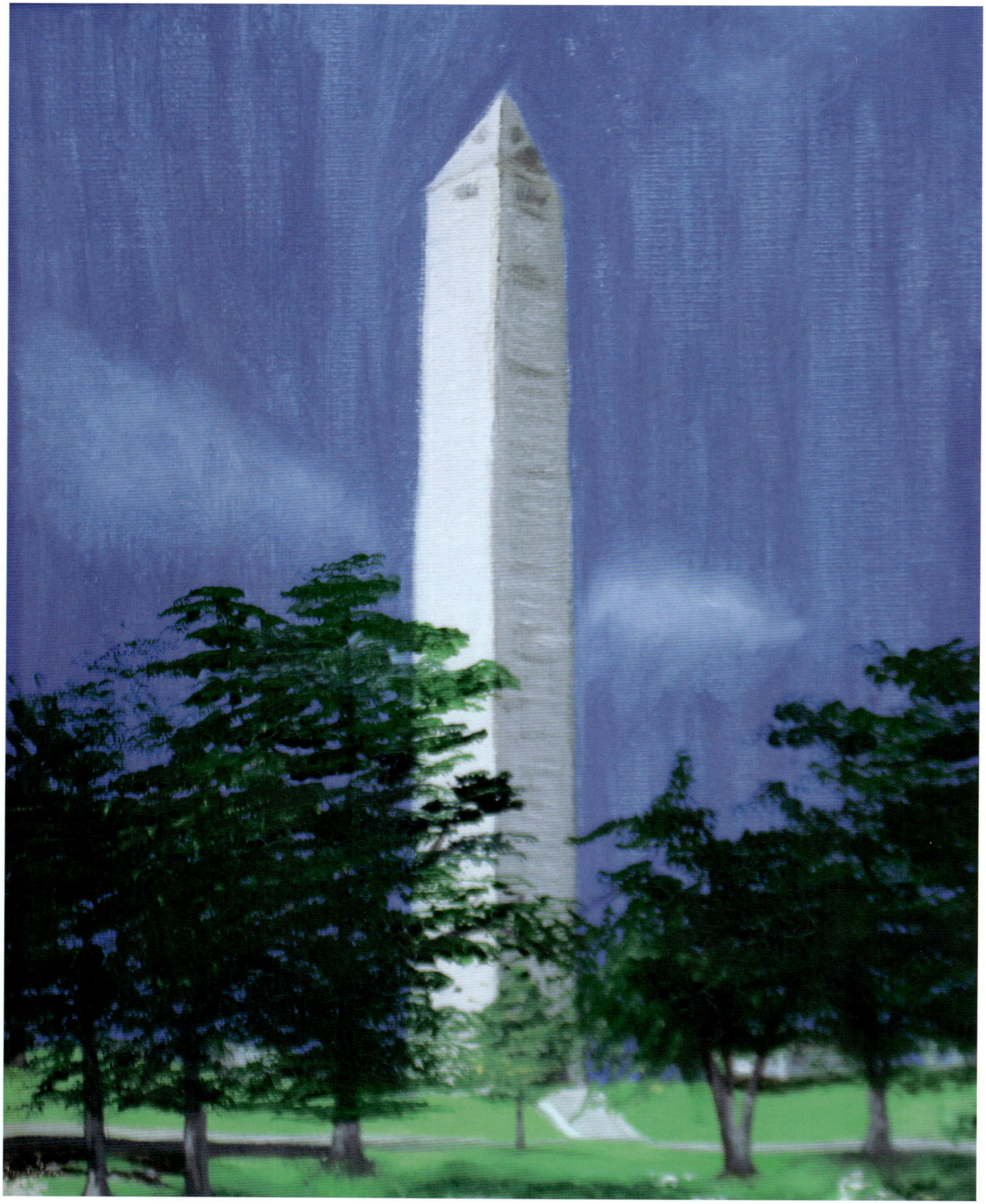

2

2 State Parks highlight the history, beauty and diverse geography that make up our home. In the south, Jefferson Davis State Historical Site overlooks fertile farmlands, and in the north, Pennyrile State Park features forested hills and hollows.

Jane Latham, artist

Sponsored By Hopkinsville-Christian County Convention and Visitors Bureau

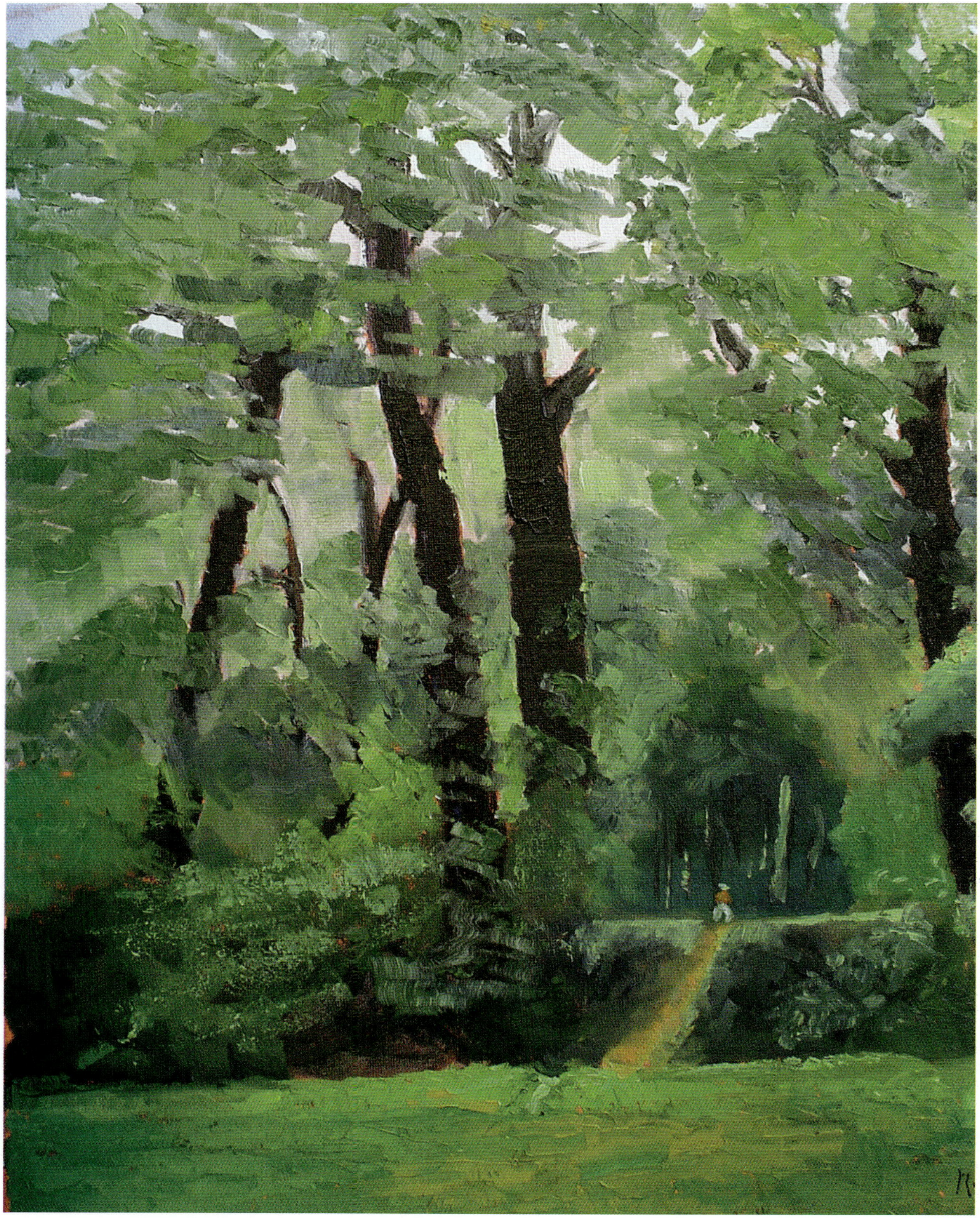

3

3 miles of walking trails meander through Jeffers Bend Botanical Garden and Environmental Center, a quiet retreat in the heart of Hopkinsville. It provides annual opportunities to experience nature through Nature Fest, Take Kids Fishing Day, Dinner by the River, Christmas at the Bend and school field days.

Nada Fuqua, artist

Sponsored By Dan and Henrietta Kemp

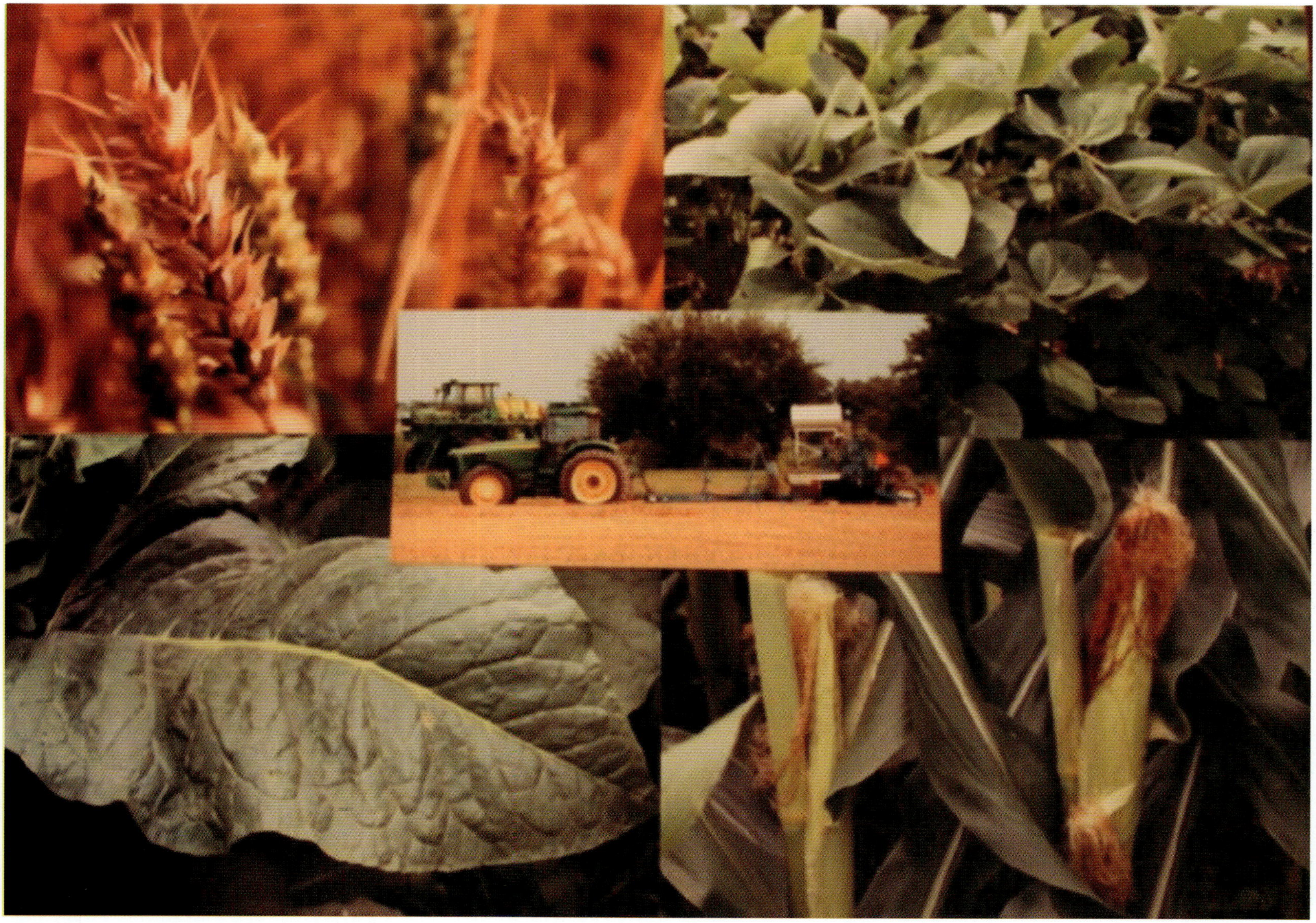

4

4 major crops have defined our way of life for generations. Every year Christian County ranks at or near the top in production in the state for wheat, soybeans, corn and tobacco.

Sharon Delaney, artist

Sponsored By Planters Bank

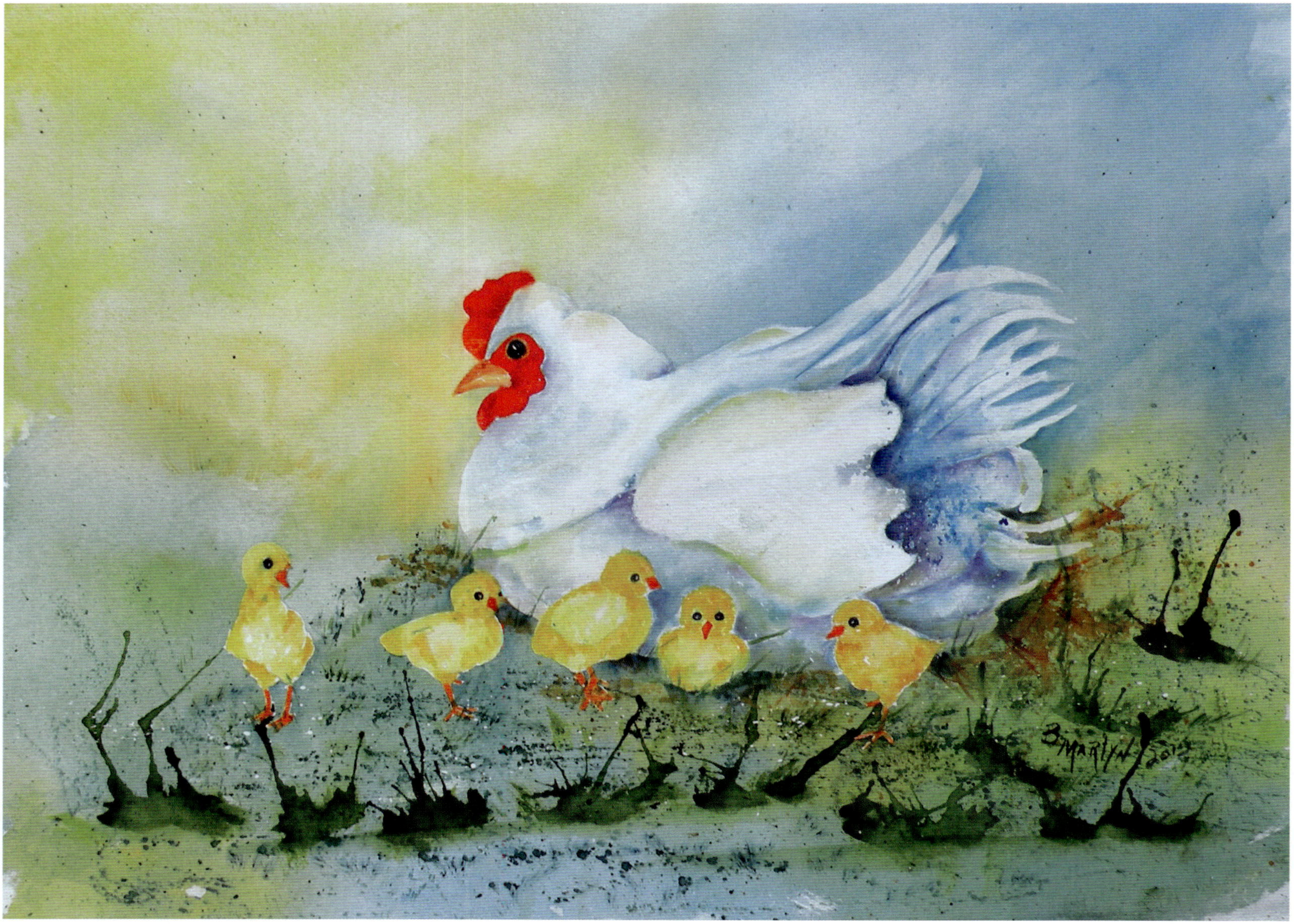
B.MARILYN

5

5 baby chicks enjoy life at the Christian Way Farms. For almost two decades families have been coming here to experience a simpler way of life. You may pick a pumpkin, take a tractor ride, and visit the farm animals.

Betty Martyn, artist

In recognition of the contributions of Bob Lancaster Designs

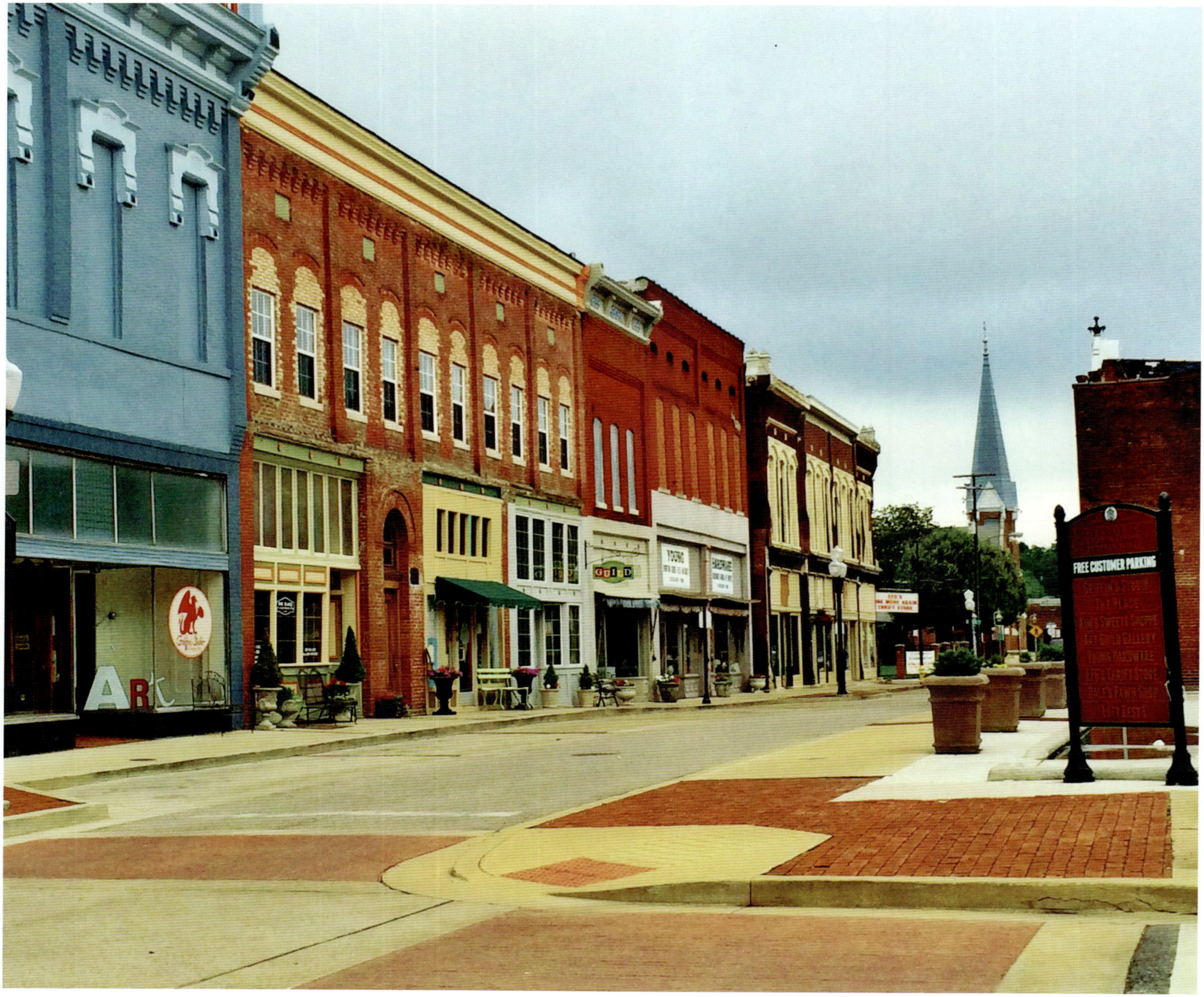
FREE CUSTOMER PARKING

6

6th Street comes alive with the arts: discover decorative and hand-crafted items at Griffin's Studio and the Hopkinsville Art Gallery, explore the art of fine eating at The Place and Kim's Pastry and Ice Cream and enjoy the art of collecting at Young's Hardware with items from yesterday and today.

Nancy Stalls, artist

Sponsored By Griffin's Studio, The Place, Kim's Sweets Shoppe, Hopkinsville Art Gallery & Young Hardware

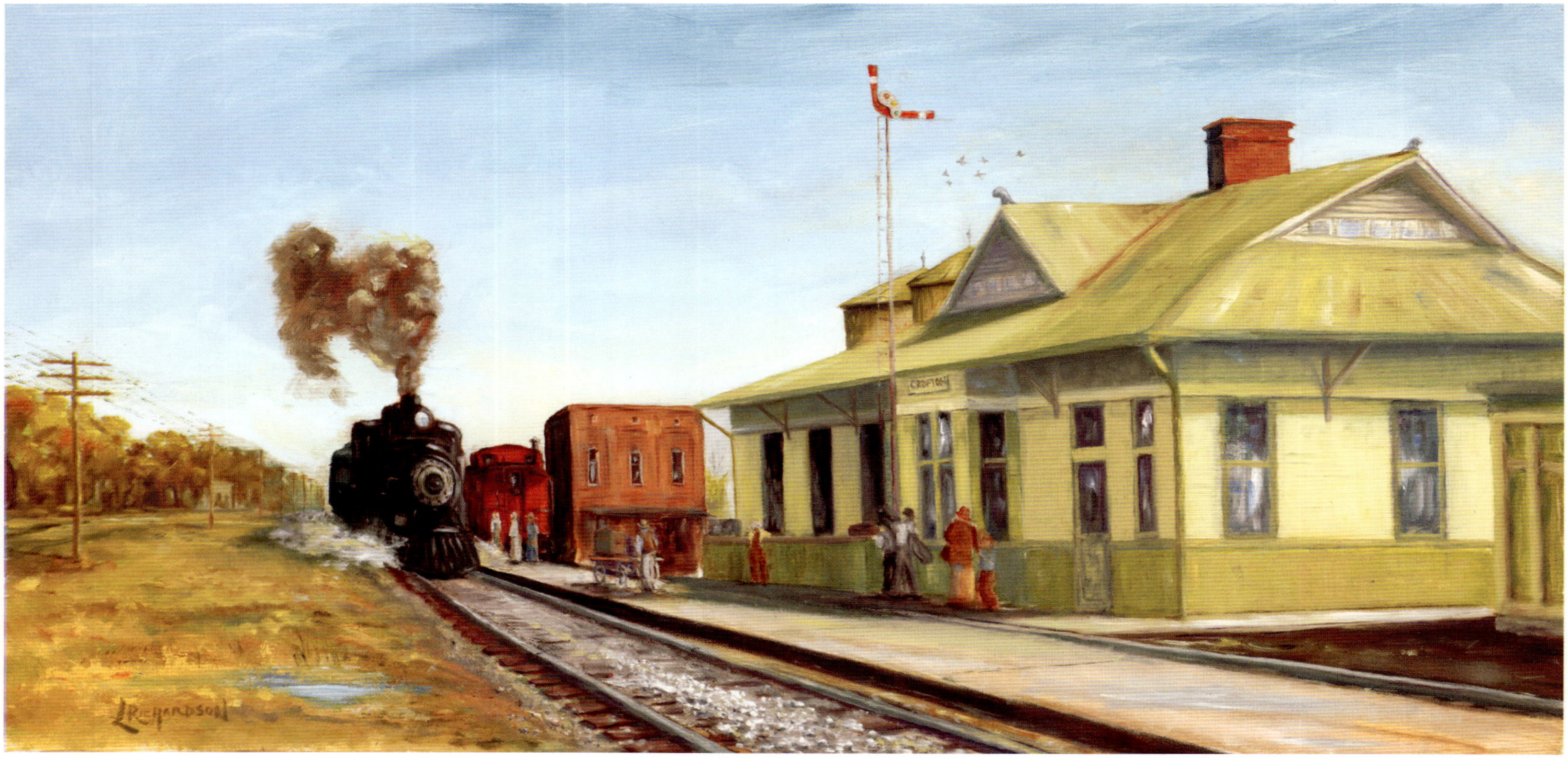
CROFTON
L RICHARDSON

7

There are 7 distinctly unique communities which make up our county, each with its own history, character and traditions. Starting with Hopkinsville in 1804, next came Oak Grove, Lafayette, Pembroke, Fairview, Crofton, and Gracey.

Larry Richardson, artist

Sponsored By Christian County Government

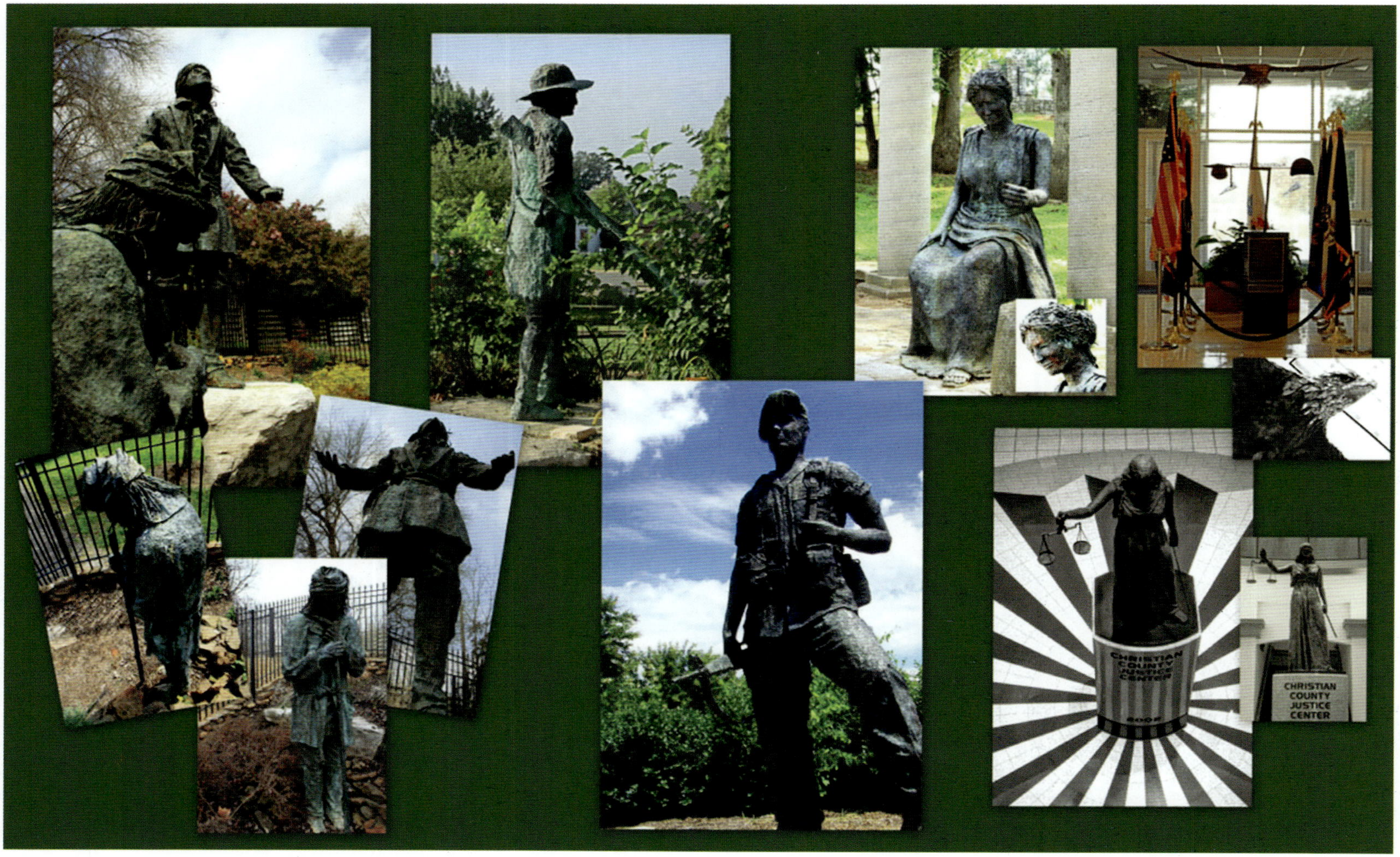
CHRISTIAN
COUNTY
JUSTICE
CENTER
2008
CHRISTIAN
COUNTY
JUSTICE
CENTER

8

8 artistic creations by Steve Shields beautify our community. One of his most moving sculptures is in Hopkinsville's Gander Memorial Park which commemorates the 248 soldiers from Fort Campbell killed in a tragic plane crash in Gander, Newfoundland, in 1985.

Angela Comperry, artist

Sponsored By Steve Shield's Family

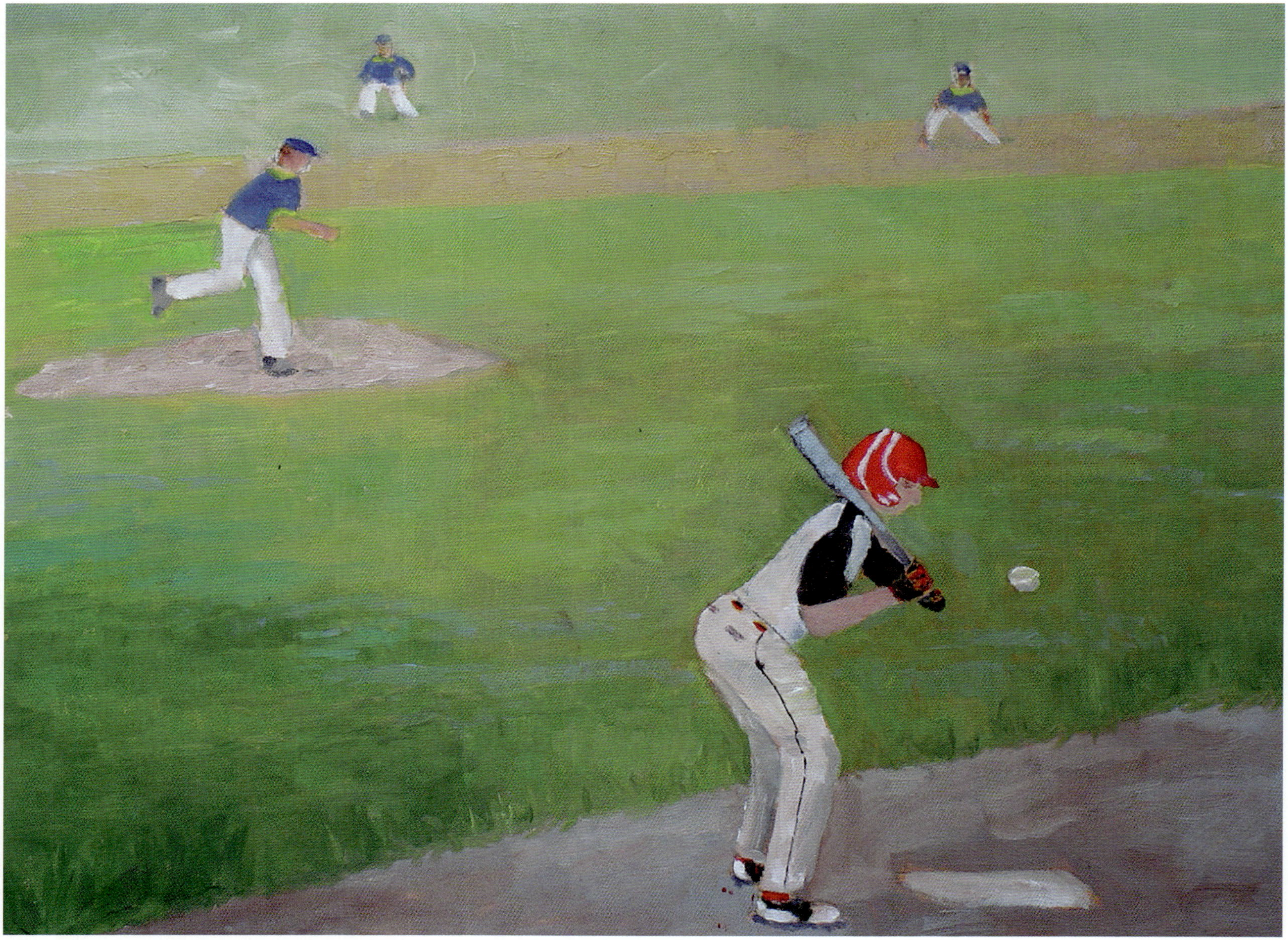

9

9 players take the field and the crack of ball against bat signals the start of another Hoptown Hoppers baseball season. Originally a minor league team from 1903 to 1955, sponsored by local businesses, the Hoppers were resurrected in 2012.
"Take me out to the ball game..."

Nada Fuqua, artist

Sponsored By Harper House

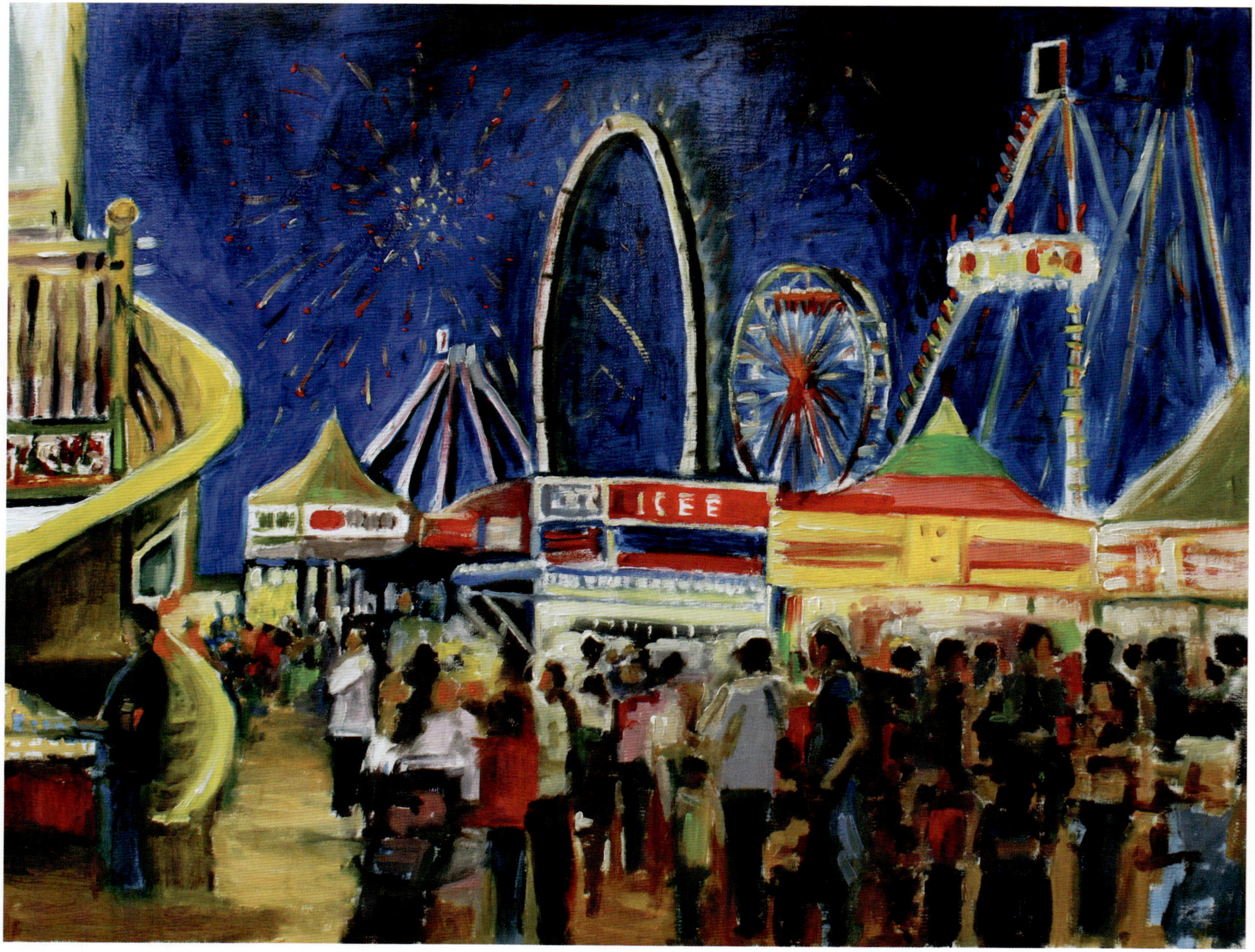
ICEE

10

10 days of summer fun make up the Western Kentucky State Fair: midway rides, funnel cakes and corndogs by night and tractor pulls, pageants and livestock exhibitions by day. Enter your pies, crafts and produce to get the blue ribbon!

Betty Liles, artist

Sponsored By the Western Kentucky Fair Board

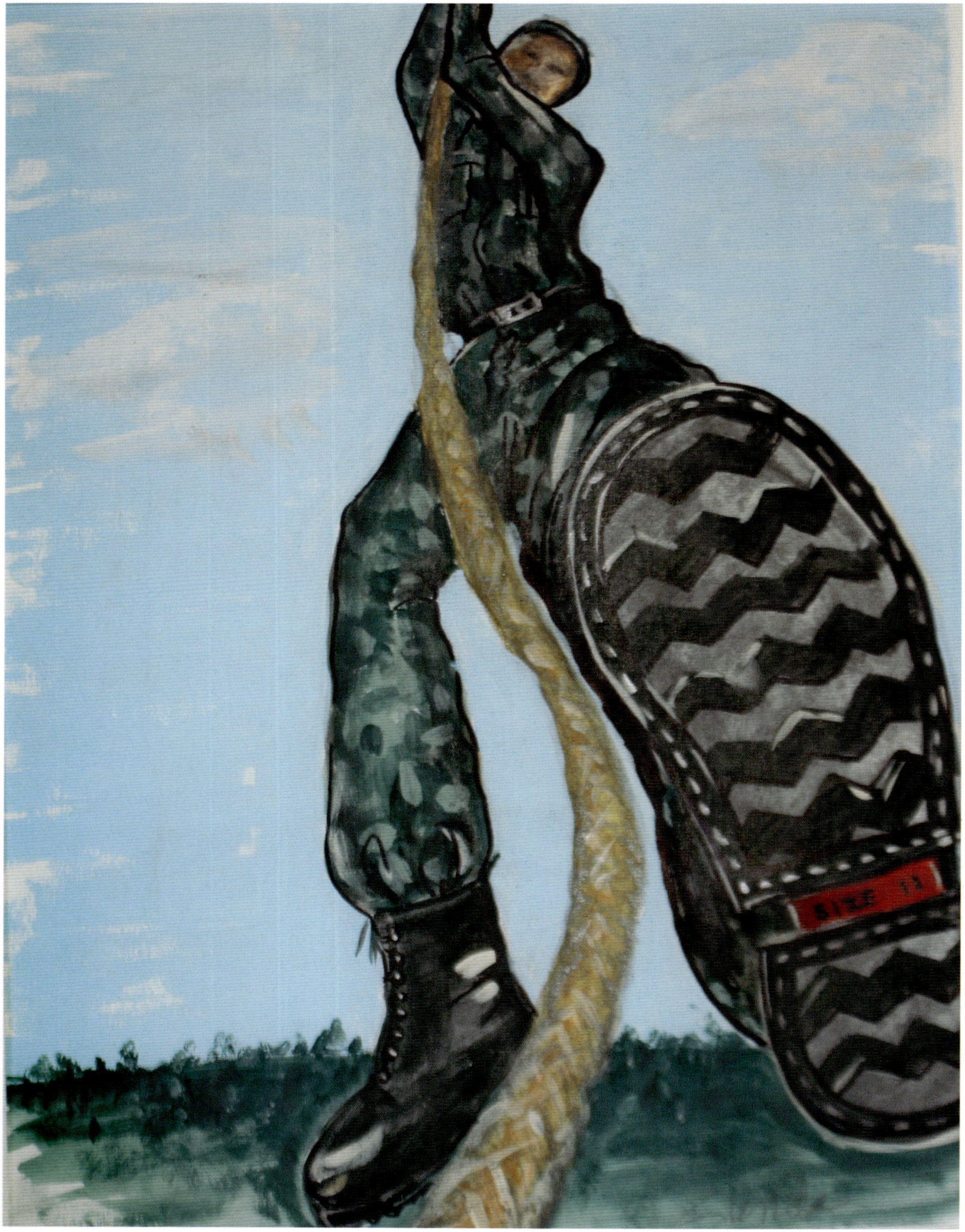

11

Size 11s land a soldier jumping from the Air Assault Rappelling Tower. Known as Camp Campbell when building began in 1942, Fort Campbell today is home to the 101st Airborne division, the only air assault division in the U. S. Army.

Glenda, artist

Sponsored By Christian County Chamber Military Affairs Committee

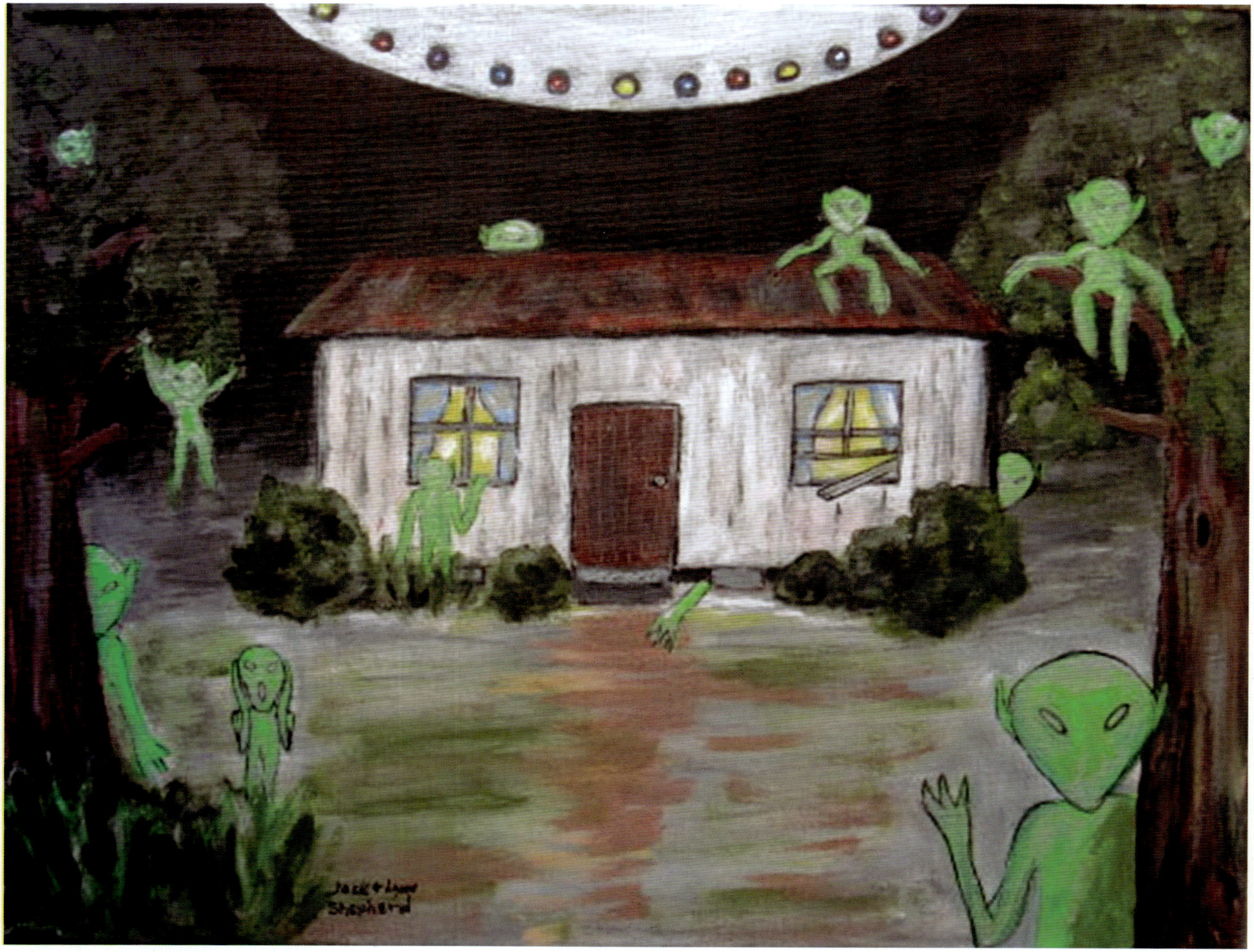
Shepherd

12

On a steamy night in August of 1955, 12 strangers and their flying saucer startled the occupants of a farmhouse in the Kelly community. They have never returned, but the Little Green Men Festival is now an annual event drawing crowds from far and near.

Jack & Lynn Shepherd, artists

Sponsored By Hopkinsville-Christian County Convention and Visitors Bureau

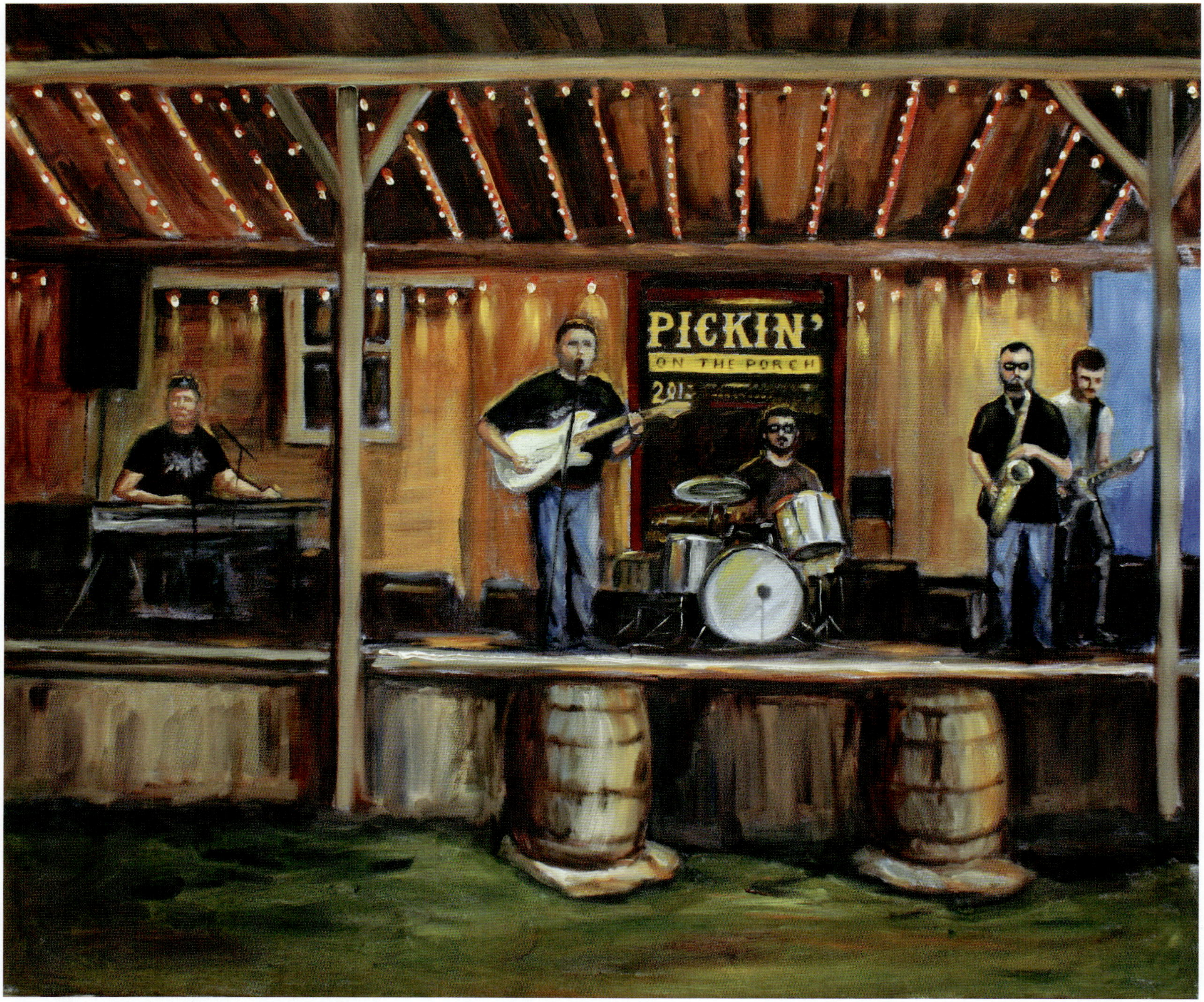
PICKIN'
ON THE PORCH

13

13 musicians tune up for a night of "Pickin' on the Porch" at the M.B. Roland Distillery, makers of small batch bourbon whiskey. Crowds gather in the field to picnic and enjoy the music on warm summer nights.

Betty Liles, artist

Sponsored By Free Range Flowers at Martin Farm

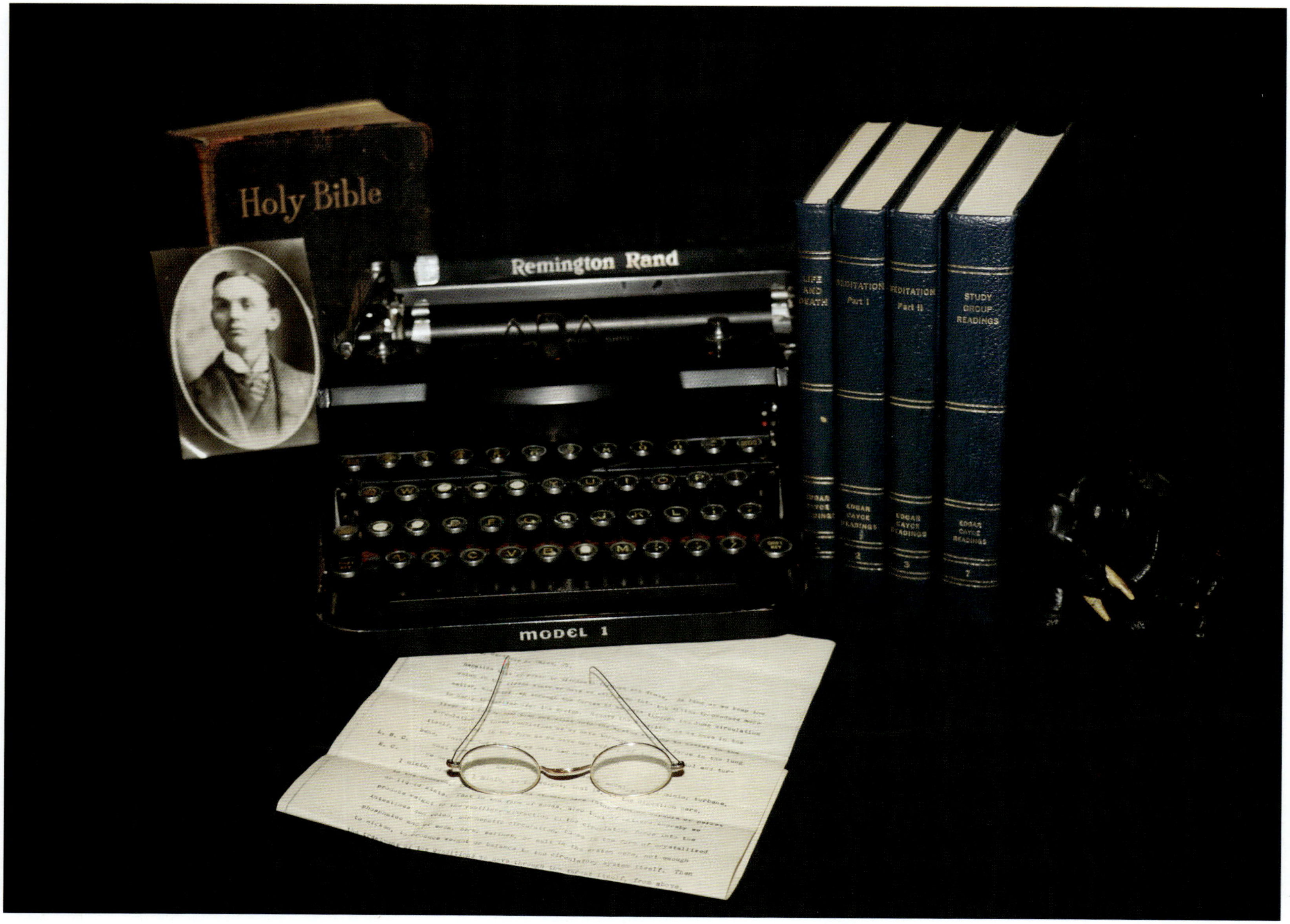
Holy Bible
Remington Rand
MODEL 1
Part I
Part II
STUDY GROUP READINGS
EDGAR CAYCE READINGS
EDGAR CAYCE READINGS

14

Known both as the "Sleeping Prophet" and father of the New Age movement, local man Edgar Cayce gave more than 14 thousand readings over his lifetime to people seeking help. This gifted psychic tapped into a level of consciousness that enabled him to guide others toward healing mind, body and soul.

Dee Anna Sova, artist

Sponsored By The Museums of Hopkinsville

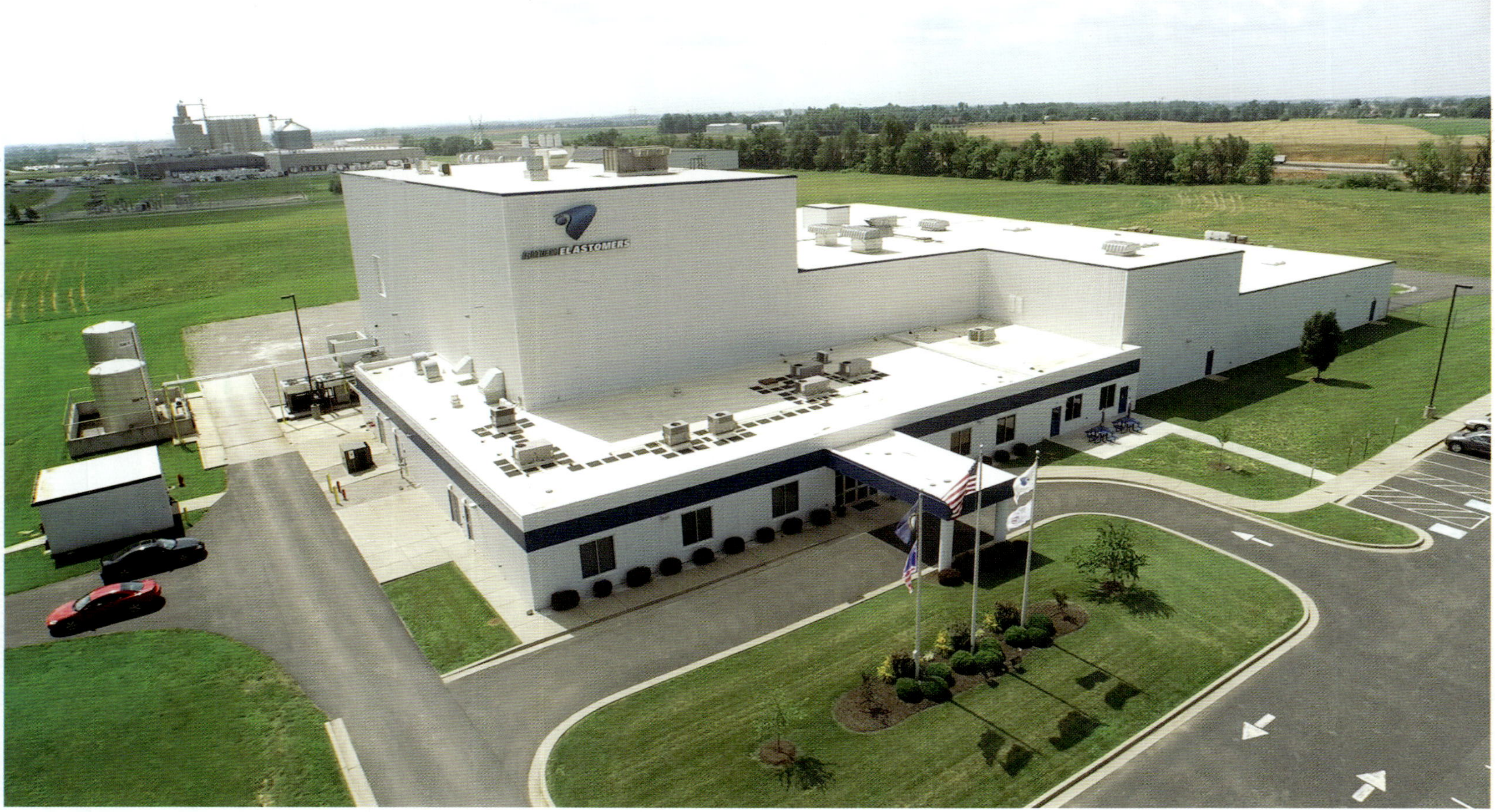
ELASTOMERS

15

15 internationally-owned industries bring new ventures and diversity to our community. Countries represented are Japan, Germany, Spain, Italy, Finland, Canada and Mexico. Each industry brings something unique to our county and provides resources used all over the world.

Dan Stahl, artist

Sponsored By South Western Kentucky Economic Development Council

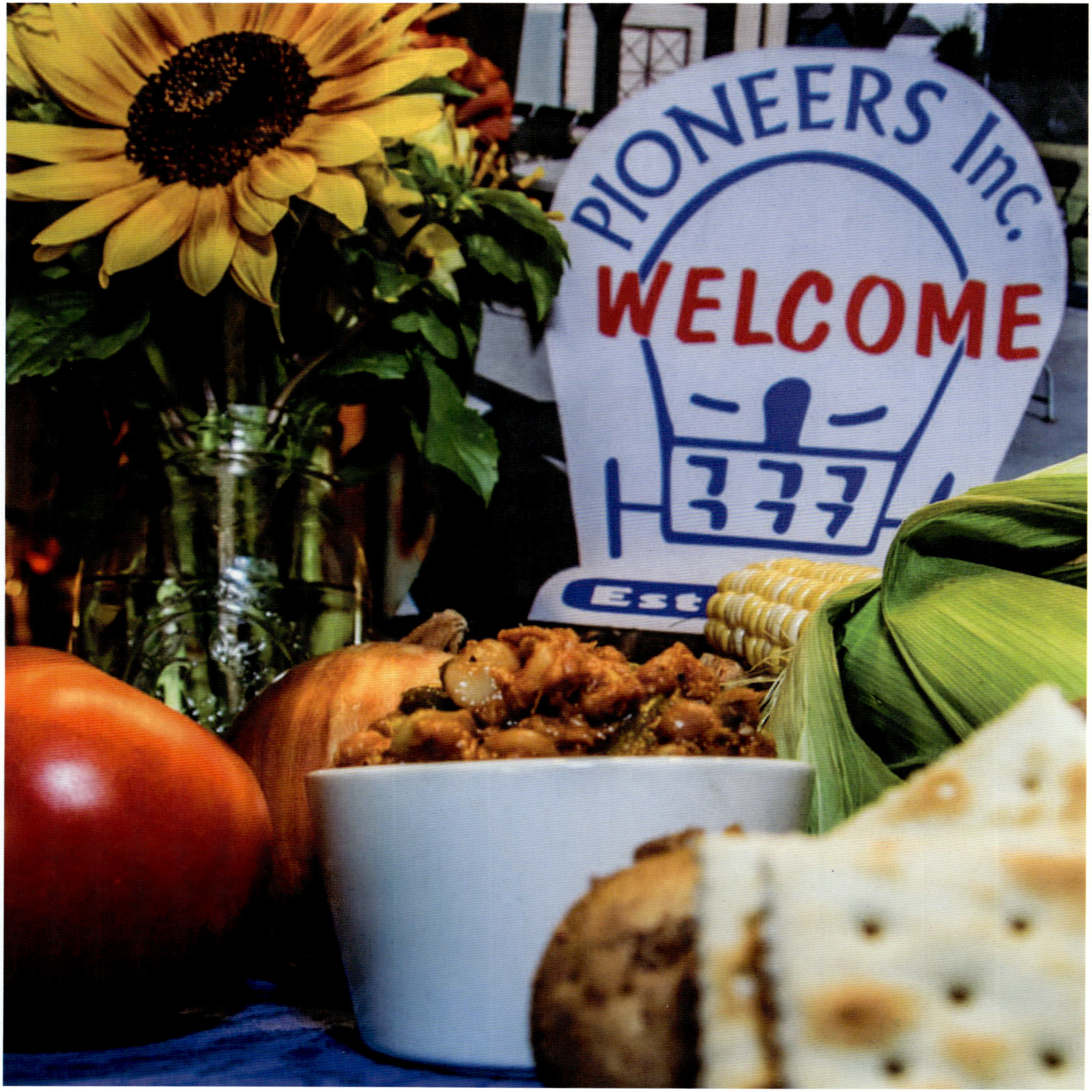
PIONEERS Inc.
WELCOME
Est

16

16 ingredients (some top secret!) make up a pot of Pioneers' burgoo. Unique to our region, this savory stew is welcome company on a cold day. This civic organization is dedicated to community service.

Margaret Prim, artist

Sponsored By Pioneers Incorporated

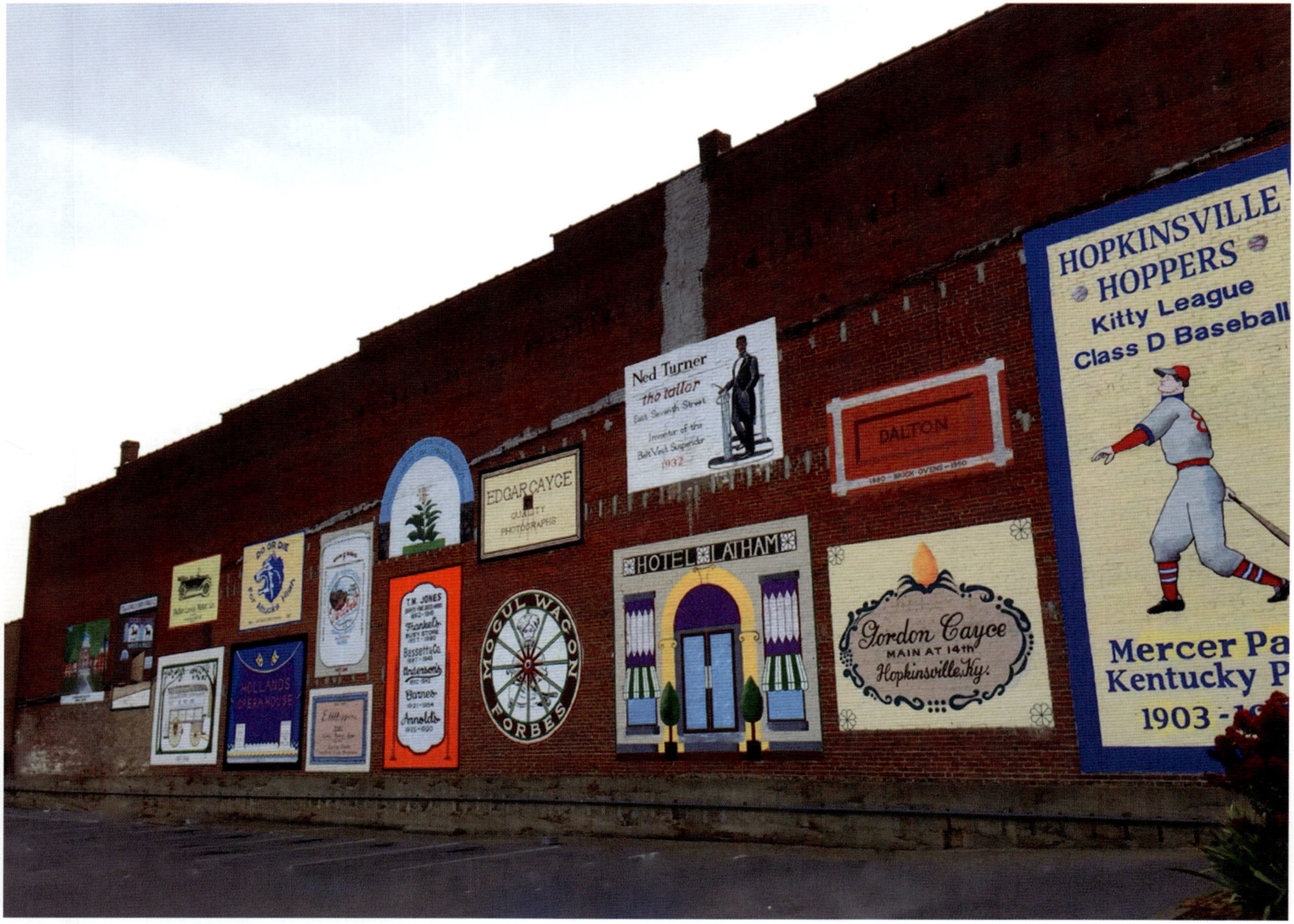
HOPKINSVILLE
HOPPERS
Kitty League
Class D Baseball
Mercer Pa
Kentucky P
1903 -
Ned Turner
the tailor
East Seventh Street
Inventor of the
Belt Vest Suspender
1932
DALTON
EDGAR CAYCE
QUALITY
PHOTOGRAPHS
HOTEL LATHAM
Gordon Cayce
MAIN AT 14th
Hopkinsville, Ky.
MOGUL WAGON
FORBES
T.M. JONES
Frankel's
Bassett & Co.
Anderson's
Barnes
Arnolds
HOLLANDS
OPERAHOUSE
DO OR DIE

17

17 murals showcasing the past overlook Founders Square in downtown Hopkinsville. The pavilion there hosts the Farmers Market in the summertime and community events throughout the year.

David White, artist

Sponsored By Hopkinsville Christian County Development Corporation

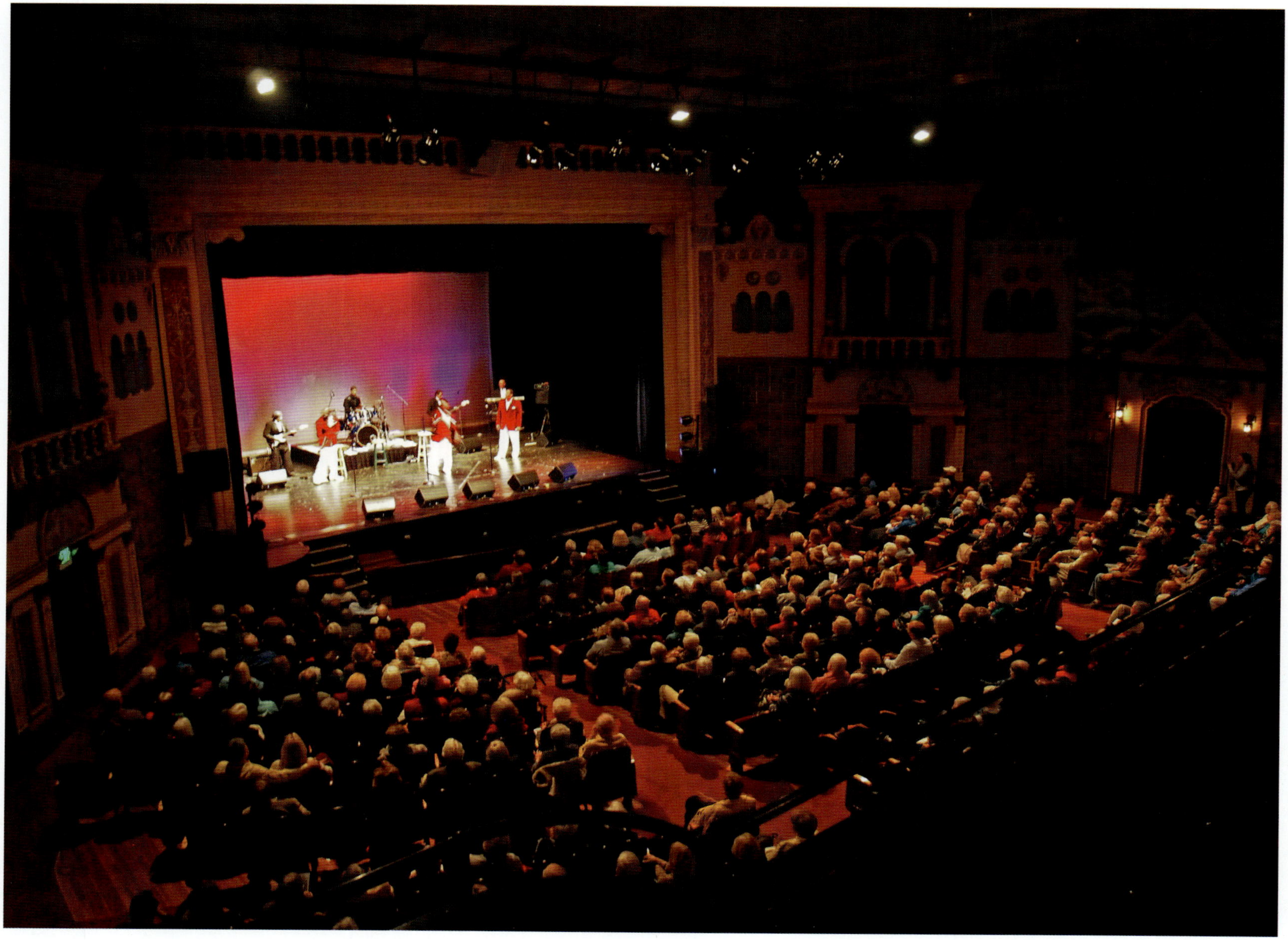

18

Choose your favorite seat from one of 18 rows in the historic Alhambra theatre. First opened in 1928, the theater is a venue for live music, comedy, drama, community theater and classic movies. The Pennyroyal Arts Council loves and cares for this building.

David White, artist

Sponsored By Hopkinsville Water Environment Authority

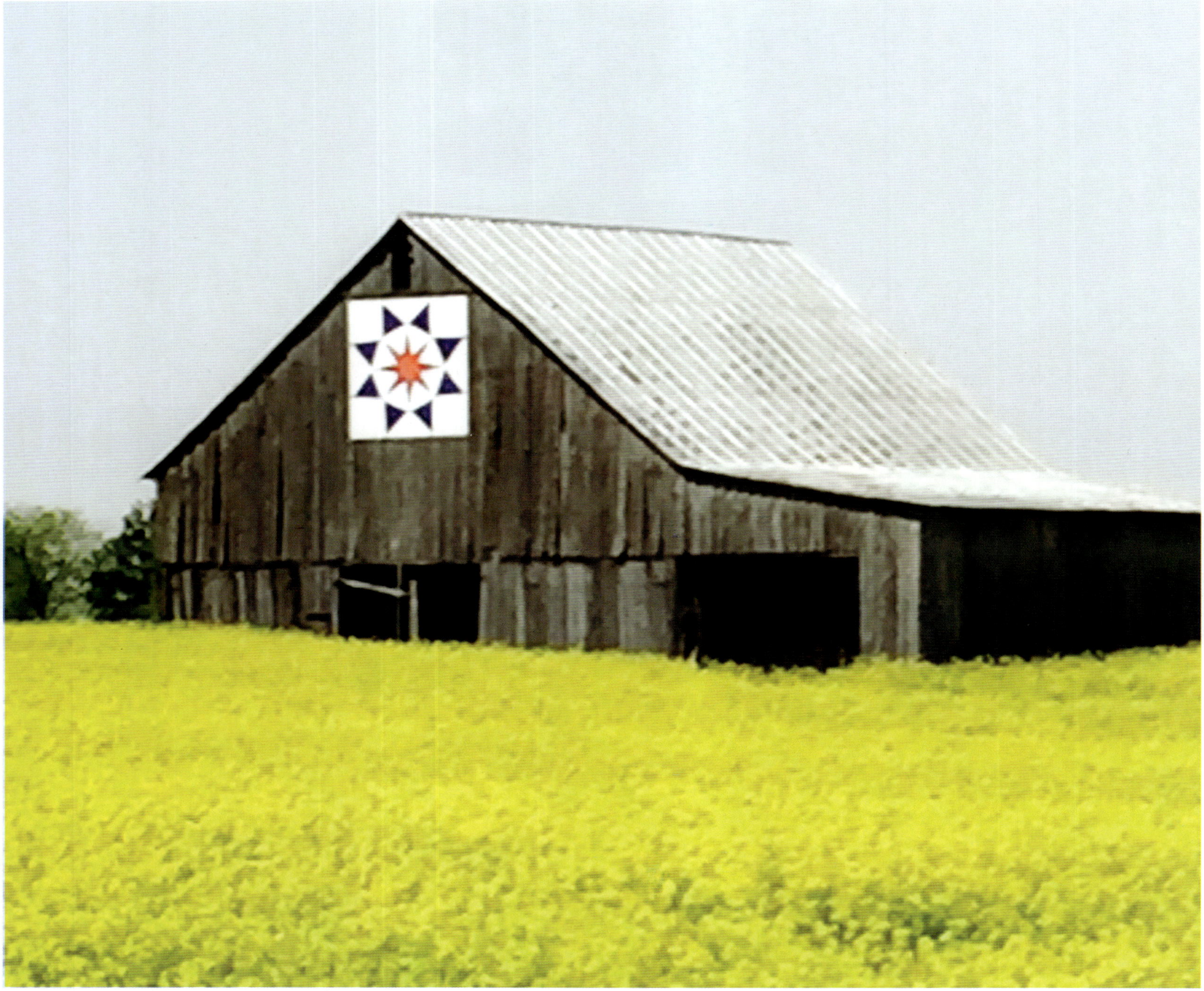

19

Quilt squares adorn the sides of 19 barns and buildings throughout the county. The colorfully painted patterns brighten the countryside and tell us stories if we pay attention. This barn, in a sea of blooming canola, uses a variation of the flying geese pattern.

Margaret Prim, artist

Sponsored By Christian County Homemakers Association

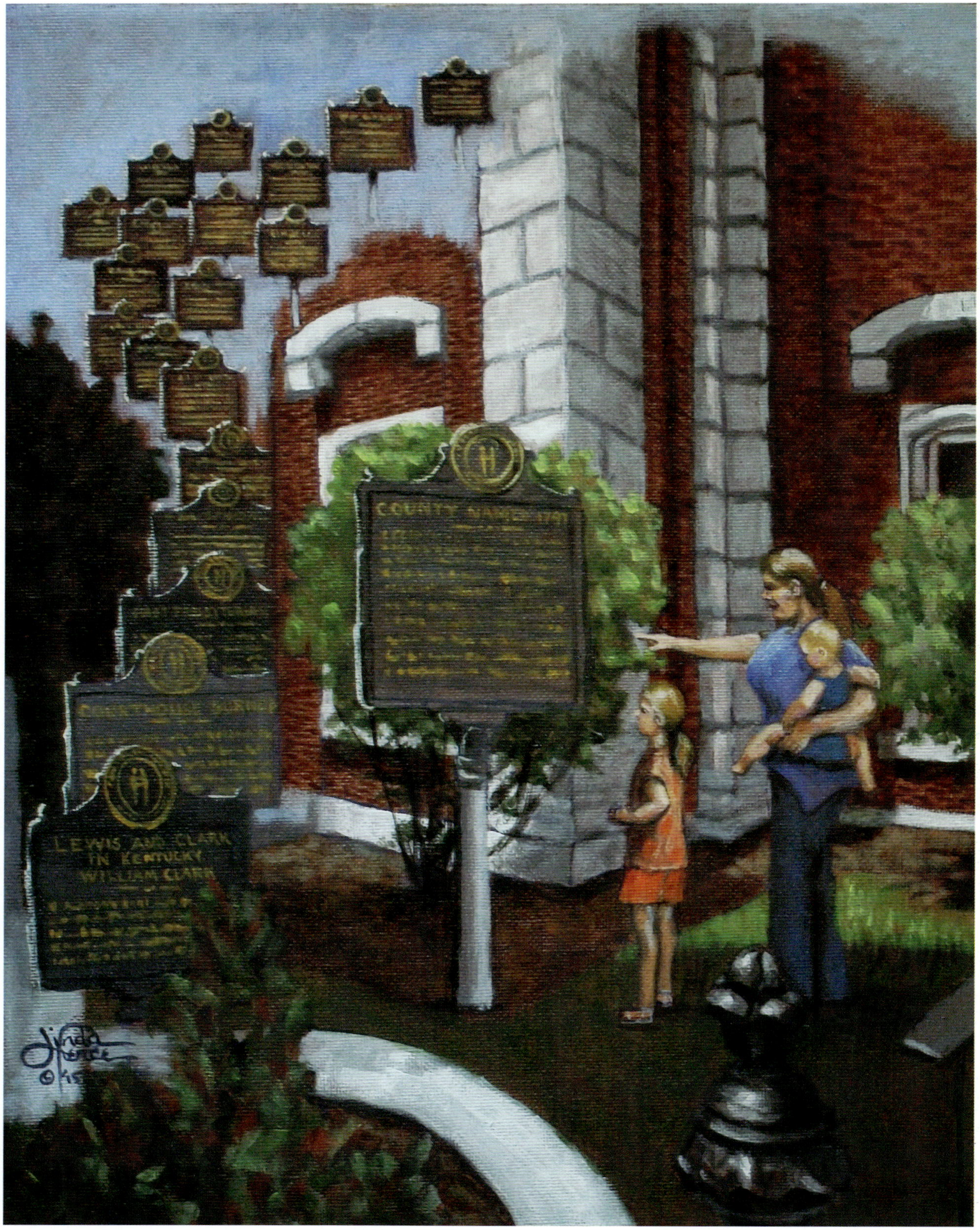
LEWIS AND CLARK
IN KENTUCKY
WILLIAM CLARK

20

20 State Historical Markers along our roads recall events from the county's past. Did you know in 1962 Christian County was at the forefront of agricultural practices and among the first in the nation to practice no-till crop production? See the spot at marker 1759.

Linda Pierce, artist

Sponsored By Christian County Historical Society

(1) MURRAY BLAKE

I am a self taught photographer and photo shop artist. I have lived in Hopkinsville for most of my life. My love of the outdoors and of the wildlife that lives all around us has helped drive my love for photography. While working the nightshift at UPS for 26 years, I spent a lot of time photographing in low light and after dark making timed exposures. After retiring from UPS I now work as a construction painter and I have more time to take photos. I also like to make and sell artwork from photos that I have taken around our local area. We are so blessed to live in this beautiful area, there is always something new and amazing to photograph.

(2) JANE LATHAM

I have drawn and sketched all my life, but never put paint on canvas until 2010 when my husband bought me paint supplies and said "Here, try painting!". I take oil painting lessons from Barbara Gardner. I love to paint buildings, old mills, landscapes and waterfalls. I hope those viewing my painting of the Jeff Davis Monument will be touched by memories it evokes as it touched my soul in painting it.

(3)(9) NADA FUQUA

Oil painting has been Nada's hobby for a long time while she has lived here in Hopkinsville. She loves the way it moves, even how it smells. As an artist she is more aware of colors, forms and light than most people. She began working with pastels a few years ago and found it was an extension of her love for drawing portraits. She has studied with Barbara Gardner, Dawn Whitelaw, Michael Shane Neal, Tony Rider, Pat Thompson, Bill Fletcher, Roger Dale Brown and Everitt Raymond Kinstler. She is a member of the Hopkinsville Art Guild and Gallery, Downtown Artists' Co-Op in Clarksville, and the Portrait Society of America.

(4) SHARON DELANEY

I am a native of Hopkinsville, Ky. I am a graduate of Hopkinsville High School, Hopkinsville Community College, and Austin Peay State University. I have a Bachelor of Science Degree in Mass Communication and a Master of Arts Degree in Education. I was a Special Education teacher for several years. Now I am pursuing my passion for art in painting, drawing, and photography. I have taken many painting classes from Linda Pierce and have learned a lot about acrylic painting. I have had art exhibited at Hopkinsville Community College, the Chamber of Commerce, and the L & N Depot. I hope to continue to learn about many other mediums through classes and workshops. I am a member of the Hopkinsville Art Guild and Gallery and hope to have art on display there soon.

(5) BETTY MARTYN

I was born and reared in Dickson County, Tennessee in a town called Bon Aqu. It is a beautiful name for a beautiful place. It is a place of hills, woods and fast running water. I loved the wild things around me then and now. I am basically a self taught artist but I have studied under several artists whose work I admire. Although I work in several mediums, watercolor is my medium of choice. The transparent, luminous quality of watercolor suits my style of painting. I belong to several arts organizations and have won several awards for my work. Art is a magnificent obsession, it is also my passion. I believe you should work at your art every day, not become stagnant and complacent in your work, keep learning and keep seeking the rainbow. It's a wonderful journey.

(6) NANCY STALLS

Cast between thought and feeling, my history in photography is a brief bio. Sunlit fields, shadowed doors, and poppy's bright; my mind's perceptions are drawn by the eye of the camera. I am a native of Murray, KY, now residing in Hopkinsville, KY. I studied the art of black and white photography at Paducah, KY Community College, developing and printing my photographs in my private darkroom. I have exhibited my works at the Yeiser Art Gallery, Paducah, KY; the Murray Art Guild Gallery, Murray, KY; the Janice Mason Art Museum, Cadiz, KY; the Bowling Green, KY Art Guild Gallery, Bowling Green, KY; and the Hopkinsville, KY Art Guild Gallery, Hopkinsville, KY. My photographs have won prizes in juried shows in all of the venues shown. I also work as a free-lance photographer and enjoy photographing senior high students, weddings, and family photos.

(7) LARRY RICHARDSON

I love to paint and I paint mostly outdoor scenes of what I enjoy. My leisure time is spent hiking, hunting, fishing, sailing, and biking. Rainy days are for painting in the studio. Born in Christian County,

Kentucky, my love of the outdoors led to a career that included an advanced degree in biology, work in parks and wildlife, art publishing, U.S. Senate and currently as a painter of scenes of "where I like to be." After retiring from Ducks Unlimited, my wife and I moved to Waverly, Tennessee. I began to consider art seriously when I worked with noted wildlife painter Ralph McDonald, helping him develop a new business in the 1970s. Since then, I have been involved in both art publishing and sales throughout my career. I guess you could say I've looked over the shoulders of a lot of great artists I've known while working in the art publishing industry. I've also had formal training. I like realism, not photographic, but more toward an impressionistic style, leaving a loose edge or the gesture of a shadow, inviting the viewer to make the final stroke. The method follows a "loose style" utilized by some of my favorite artists like Winslow Homer, Thomas Eakin, John Singer Sargent, Frank Benson and others who employ that genre. I paint for my own enjoyment and if others like what's on the canvas, then it's even more enjoyable for me. I try to keep a painting on the easel and work on something daily.

(8) ANGELA COMPERRY

I have liked photography since way back in the days of film, but began to do a lot more of it when digital cameras came along and I could make lots of mistakes at no expense. My passion for it really developed when I joined the online Amateur Photography Contest Group with a talented group of mostly Canadian photographers. I was critiqued weekly by Canadians Doreen Hollett, Jim Cornish, Brent van Hooft, Nashville photographer Gwen Meacham and others. Thinking my photos were winners, they quickly pointed out that my horizons were slanted, my contrast was wrong, my colors were off, I was overexposed, underexposed, full of distractions, noisy and not on the thirds. Thankfully, they didn't kick me out of their group and they taught me most of what I know or told me where to find the answer. I have a special affection for all of those people. Outdoor photography became my thing, and since there are no mountains or ocean here in Crofton, Kentucky, I decided I would make the most of my surroundings photographing rural landscapes. I needed a focal point, so why not barns. They came in lots of shapes and colors, with a history and added nicely to the landscapes. And there were beautiful farms and crops and lakes and forests and old buildings and all things associated with them and so I developed my style as a photographer. I won some contests. My photos were chosen for calendars and hung in City Hall. Jim Monroe sold my photos as art at Statons Art and Framing. Strangers bought my photos and hung them in their homes. I even went outside my comfort zone and did a C.D. cover for a country music singer. I feel "famous in a small town." So I'll keep learning and challenging myself and see where it goes. Every day is a new search for that perfect photo when everything comes together and makes me happy.

(10)(13) BETTY LILES

I was born and raised in Christian County, Kentucky, and studied commercial and fine art at Austin Peay State University. I completed graduate work in studio painting at Murray State University. I also hold degrees in Business Administration and a Master of Arts in Education. I retired after 31 years of college teaching and have devoted my time to furthering my art education by attending art workshops all over the country including the Art Students League in New York City. I have exhibited in many art shows throughout the region and won several awards for my paintings and drawings including being selected to exhibit at the Kentucky State Capitol in Frankfort, Kentucky. My work can be seen at the Guild Gallery, Griffins', and Staton's Art & Framing in Hopkinsville, Kentucky; the Downtown Artists' Co-op and Silke's Old World Bakery in Clarksville, Tennessee; and on my web site at www.BettyPierceLiles.com . I enjoy painting or drawing a variety of subjects in various medias, including oil, acrylic, watercolor, pastels, graphite, and mixed media. I am a member of the Downtown Artists' Co-op, the Hopkinsville Art Guild/Gallery, Women Painters of the Southeast, and the Portrait Society of America. I welcome commissions of any type and teach art work-shops and private lessons upon request.

(11) GLENDA

I have a degree in Art Therapy and a degree in Art Education with a minor of Studio Art. My education took place at Milwaukee Institute of Art and Design, Alverno College in Milwaukee, Marquette University and Art Institute of Chicago. I have completed masters work in Art Therapy and Education. My love of discovery and the ability to think outside of the box was fostered at Alverno where I graduated with honors. I worked in public schools with troubled kids and adults and spent many years teaching at alternative schools. I have traveled extensively within the United States and Europe. Those experiences helped me to accept differing cultures and alternative methods of creativity. I lived in Mexico for many years. That experience really helped to bridge the gap of creativity within poverty and how to create art with what you have. I began to see the possibilities of discovering history thru using materials that were left behind. I believe my studies of spirituality and religion expanded what my focus is now: Creativity as prayer. As an artist I want to bring art to those people who don't necessarily have a chance to experience it. I want to change the minds of people about what art is. I want to be a bridge for them so that they may embrace their own creativity.

(12) JACK & LYNN SHEPHERD

We are both natives of Christian County and remember well the "Little Green Men" incident. We were away for more than 25 years in which time Jack graduated from The George Washington University and retired as Lieutenant Commander in the U.S. Navy Medical Service Corps. Lynn's formal education in sociology and rehab counseling culminated at the University of Memphis. Since Jack's Navy retirement, we were realtors in Memphis and Hoptown. Now retired from all careers, we enjoy being members of the Hopkinsville Art Guild and Gallery where Jack paints primarily acrylic abstracts while Lynn's efforts are more impressionistic/realistic. Both of us exhibit and sell at the Hopkinsville Art Gallery.

(14) DEEANNA SOVA

I have called Hopkinsville, KY my home since 2010. I have been an avid photographer for nearly 25 years and especially enjoy classic black and white images. I have a Bachelor of Science Degree in Business Administration from Austin Peay State University and am involved in a number of community organizations, including the Hopkinsville Art Guild. When I am not photographing, I serve as the Director of the Occupational Health Clinic & Community Engagement at Jennie Stuart Medical Center. I am married to Paul Sova, and am most proud of my family, daughter and son-in-law, Drew and Chris Howes, parents to my grandson, Jackson, and my son and daughter-in-law, Davin and Kayla Ramage.

(15) DANIEL STAHL

I am the owner/operator of CCPro Video located in Hopkinsville, Christian County. CCPro Video specializes in video production and graphical design elements. Aerial photography has added a new dimension to CCPro Video's arsenal with 4K digital film quality and rapid production time at an economical cost to the consumer. I have a background in the military, a BS in Political Science and a MS in Public Administration. I have worked for the Christian County Chamber of Commerce and the Kentucky New Era as Web and Graphics Technology Director. CCPro Video is happy to contribute to the Pennyroyal Arts Council's and Hopkinsville Art Guild's book this year with aerial footage of Riken Elastomers, one of Christian County's vital industrial park partners.

(16) CATHERINE LACY

I am a 25 year old native Kentuckian from Todd County. As a recent University of Kentucky grad, I reside in Lexington working as a freelance videographer and photographer. My aspiration of becoming a music video and commercial videographer to the stars has led to my abundant creativity.

(17)(18) DAVID WHITE

I am a native of Hopkinsville, Kentucky, a graduate of Hopkinsville High School and the University of North Carolina at Chapel Hill. I have lived in Ft. Lauderdale, Gulfport, New Orleans and Nashville. Upon retiring from a 40 year career in healthcare, I moved back home to Hopkinsville. I have recently taken up photography and provide some of my work to the Pennyroyal Arts Council. You can often find me and my dog Skeeter walking on the Rail Trail or out at Jeffers Bend.

(19) MARGARET PRIM

I am now beginning my third year as the Executive Director of the Pennyroyal Arts Council and am excited about being at the helm at a crucial time for the future of the creative community. I am also the owner of The Perfect Closet and have represented Worth, an up-scale women's clothing line, for thirteen years. I am the food columnist for the Kentucky New Era and my column, "What's on the Menu" runs the first Wednesday of each month. My husband Tony and I live in Hopkinsville with our 2 cats, Louise and Larry. We love to cook together and entertain family and friends. I am an active member of Grace Episcopal Church.

(20) LINDA PIERCE

I am a freelance artist, instructor, and author with nearly 30 years experience. I have been working in pastels, acrylics, colored pencils, and Genesis oils. I enjoy creating portraits of people and pets, historical architecture, and nature. I also do decorative painting and murals on location or canvas murals in my studio. I view my art as a gift from the Lord, whom I credit as my primary teacher. For the past 20 years I have hosted private and group art classes. A biology major, I have nearly 20 years experience as a teacher. I have also had careers as a newspaper editor, photographer, and a dietary supervisor. A Louisville, KY native, I have resided in Hopkinsville since 1981.

(COVER) PAULA GIESEKE

Paula Gieseke is a professional artist who has lived in Kentucky most of her life. She resides at her Blue Springs Studio in Cerulean, KY and is an art teacher at Christian County High School. She is a national board certified teacher who received degrees from Austin Peay State University, Murray State University and Western Kentucky University. Paula has won numerous art awards for portrait drawings, mixed media, painting, and photography. She also serves as the Gifted and Talented Coordinator, yearbook sponsor, prom sponsor, art club sponsor, and program review coordinator for Christian County High School. She serves as the Youth Art Month district-wide exhibition coordinator, Pennyroyal Arts Council Board member, Hopkinsville Art Guild member and a KYAEA member. Paula was named the Kentucky Art Education Association High School Art Teacher of the Year for 2015 and has been nominated for the National Art Education Association Southeastern Regional High School Art Teacher of the Year for 2016 by The KYAEA. Paula designed and created the front and back cover art work for the book. It was created using a colored pencil drawing of block numbers with a map of Christian County in the center.

(BOOK DESIGN) GRIFFIN BLANE MOORE

Griffin Blane Moore is a native of Hopkinsville, Kentucky. She received her Bachelor of Fine Arts in Packaging Design from the Fashion Institute of Technology in New York City in 2009 and her Master of Arts in Teaching from Austin Peay State University in 2011. For the past several years, Griffin has been a freelance artist and graphic designer as well as a high school art teacher. She is now the owner of Griffin's Studio in Hopkinsville where she works on her art, teaches classes, and manages the shop.

About the Pennyroyal Arts Council

The mission of the Pennyroyal Arts Council is to encourage, develop, and promote the appreciation of the arts through education, support, service and presentation.

The Pennyroyal Arts Council began July 19, 1977. For the past 38 years the Arts Council has been embracing the arts for a diverse community. In 2008 restoration was completed of the historic Alhambra Theatre making it one of the region's finest performance spaces. In 2013, the Arts Council brought film back to our theatre. The Arts Council presents the LIVE at the Alhambra seasonal performances of outstanding drama, dance, and music by acclaimed regional, national and international artists. Each year through our Students Meeting the Arts Program (smARTS), the Arts Council introduces thousands of students to live dramatic productions and post-performance discussions. The Arts Council celebrates and encourages local student artists by sponsoring the annual Young Masters Art Exhibit and reception at the Hopkinsville Community College. It also works with community organizations that provide local theatre productions and great annual events like the Pennyrile Polar Express, which merges art and literacy with the holiday spirit- our way of celebrating art, family, and community.

From the Alhambra Theatre to the classroom, the Pennyroyal Arts Council has a strong commitment to education and the cultural reputation of the region.

PENNYROYAL ARTS C·O·U·N·C·I·L

Proceeds from the sale of this book and half the sales of corresponding artwork will help underwrite the educational programs and services of The Pennyroyal Arts Council and the Hopkinsville Art Guild.

Pennyroyal Arts Council is a 501(c)3 non-profit organization
L&N Depot-425 East 9th St-Hopkinsville, KY 42241
www.pennyroyalarts.org-270-887-4295

The Kentucky Arts Council, the state arts agency, supports the Pennyroyal Arts Council with state tax dollars and federal funding from the National Endowment for the Arts.

The Pennyroyal Arts Council and the Hopkinsville Art Guild thanks everyone who helped "compose" this wonderful book!

Christian County Counts: Co-Chairs, Henrietta Kemp and Margaret Prim, Betty Vinson, Carolyn Self, Yasamin Ausenbaugh, Alissa Keller, and Martha White
Additional Assistance: Doris Anne Russell, The Kentucky New Era, and Grace Episcopal Church
Book Designed By: Griffin Blane Moore/Griffin's Studio
Cover Designed By: Paula Gieseke